BLISSFUL LIVING

DESIGNING A HOME & LIFE YOU LOVE

ASHLINA KAPOSTA

Illustrations by Wenna Privé

BLISSFUL LIVING

www.thedecorista.com

ISBN-13: 978-1540467713

MADE WITH LOVE

To America, my grandmother.

Thank you for teaching us all what family means, how to love unconditionally and most importantly how to really live! We were all so incredibly lucky to experience this life with you. May your glamorously perfect little legacy forever live through the words that fill these pages.
Forever and more, I love you.

contents:

"Interiors are a natural projection of the soul." - Coco Chanel

INTRODUCTION

Have you ever felt like your home could be a little bigger, but a lack of funds makes that feel overwhelming? Do you find yourself on Friday night with nothing to wear, but never make it shopping because you aren't at your goal weight just yet? Do you ever feel like no one you know truly gets you?

Let me let you in on a little secret, you aren't alone. We are all looking to improve our lives in one way or another. Each and every one of us has a specific purpose on this earth and our lives are all about progress, not perfection. We continue to grow, expand and improve ourselves until we leave this world. Life isn't meant to be hard, it's meant to be fun and blissful.

What if I told you that the power to design the life of your dreams lies right behind your front door? Everything you want to achieve in life is possible and available for you. The best part is, it all begins at home. You see, your home is a physical expression of your current life status, a projection of what is happening in your soul. Your dreams, your fears and frustrations, what makes you laugh and what makes you cry. The four walls of your home absorb it all and they don't lie.

Take a look around at your home and see how it makes you feel. Perhaps you feel exhausted and stressed out, anxious and alone. If you aren't able to sit inside your home and experience radiant bliss, then chances are, you aren't living the life of your dreams. The most important thing for you to understand is that you alone hold the keys to the home and life of your dreams. You can achieve anything you desire, as long as you make the choice.

"Go confidently in the direction of your dreams." - Henry David Thoreau

I am going to show you how you can design a life and a home that inspires you, lights you up and makes you feel like a million bucks. Even if you are one of the lucky ones and your life is just perfect and already filled with bliss, I'm going to bet that you are looking for something new, something to inspire you or take you even higher. This is why I am writing this book. To be your cheerleader and friend, to open your eyes to the endless and beautiful potential you have in creating a beautiful life. For some of you, this is a little wake up call. It's time you start making the most of your life this very minute.

As we age, we begin to realize just how precious life is and we mustn't waste one minute of experiencing all of its glory. As technology creates new innovations, we see others as they share their lives through social media, creating beautiful imagery, not only as a means to make money, but as a way of living. Whether you are looking to increase your bank account balance, look better in your little black dress, attract your soulmate or just to experience more bliss, I want to show you how you can improve your life simply by shifting around the things in your home.

So sit back, light a candle, pour a glass of champagne so together we can go on a journey. Consider me your decor therapist. I'm going to help you unleash your potential, design a life you absolutely love and enjoy the experience of domestic bliss along the way.

A little bit about me...

I didn't just want to write another book on how to decorate. There are a million books and blogs that teach a variety of ways to style your home. The truth is, there is more to a home than the perfect chair or accent table. An interior is a canvas where you tell your story to the world.

The power of the interior was something I recognized at an early age. For me, it all started with a can of paint. I can remember the first time I was allowed to paint my bedroom. I painted my walls a deep shade of blue, which everyone hated except me. I never will forget how fabulous that room made me feel every time I walked into it. It was my own little sanctuary, the place where I could be completely myself. I felt powerful and alive. I was home. Today, my walls are slathered in black satin paint and I have never felt more complete, at ease and in a constant state of bliss when in my sacred space.

What do your
walls say
about you?

In my years as an interior designer, I have come to know my clients as more than just clients but as dear friends. Together, we embark on a journey to set the stage for the life that they want to live. When you help create a home for someone, you help create their dreams. Not only do I care that my clients have gorgeous spaces, I care that the spacing of their furniture has a good flow, that the environment is not just a room but an experience that delights their particular senses. I care that their deepest needs are met through their surroundings. I have seen my clients start new streams of income from their home, I have helped get my girls glowing from radiant health at home and I have even helped create sanctuaries that enabled couples to grow their family.

This is more than a book about interior design.

This is more than a book about interior design. I'm going to introduce you to new ways to sync up your life and your home: mind, body and soul. We are going to create your sanctuary, your respite, a home that nurtures you and supports you in being the best version of yourself. A place that makes you feel vibrant, powerful and alive while calming you, caring for you and being the comfort you have been looking for. I believe deep down to my core that when you make changes to your home, its effects vibrate throughout your entire life. Painting your walls, hanging new lights, buying fresh flowers, picking out new pillows are all steps that put you on a new path. This is one of the best ways to love yourself. When you bring intentionality into your home in how you decorate it and build it, your life will start to look like a beautiful piece of art. It's kind of like getting a new haircut or getting your nails done, it illuminates you and gives you a little bit of extra confidence to bring the best version of you out into the world.

Are you ready to design the life you've always dreamed of? Let's go!

This is your space
An oasis where you can relax
take off your shoes
enjoy yourself and the art of living
feel free, think big, think small
take your time and breathe
sense the moment, use your key
and open your heart
laugh, cry or be crazy if you like

this is your space

unknown

The Mind:

setting yourself up for wild success

Clearing out the clutter.

Let's get real. How many glamorous lives do you follow on social media on people who seem to have it all? The home, the bags, the shoes, the hair, the perfect body. You endlessly stalk their photos just to catch a glimpse and get lost in their fairy tale world? I get it. Trust me, I have been there. We all do it. What I want you to realize is that all the stalking is cluttering up your mind. You are essentially comparing your life to someone else's idea of perfection. You are thinking about, wishing for, and planning to get things that exist in the lives of people that you don't even know. This is a mindset that just sets you up for failure, because no matter what you have, it will never be enough. In a day and age where the lifestyles of the rich and beautiful are readily available for anyone to view, more people than ever now use prescription drugs. These meds have now made the number one spot in leading causes of death in the United States. It's a pretty scary thing to think about.

So why are we all so depressed?

I began to notice how often I would take on the role of therapist in so many of my clients lives. I came to know each and every client's relationship problems, frustrations and deep desires. Soon, I realized that no matter how rich you are or how seemingly perfect your life is, there is always something missing. There is always something that's driving you, something that you want but don't have. Always.

What if we decided it was time to stop watching the Kardashians and get out there and live our own fabulous life? How about instead of scrolling through Instagram, we spend our free time taking a road trip for the day and discovering something new? When was the last time you asked yourself what you really need, without the input of anyone else?

Perfection isn't real. It's just an illusion. Besides, what's perfect for you, may not be perfect for someone else. You have to take the time to discover what works best for you and your family. Your dream life shouldn't look like anybody else's.

We often only look at what's missing: the dream home, the husband, the friendships, the money, etc. While it's very important to understand that the things we desire are important to us, spending too much time dwelling on what is missing is the very thing that is holding you back from experiencing bliss right now. You do not have to have the "perfect" life to live in bliss. It begins with appreciating and making the most of what you have right now. Once you have cleaned out the mental clutter and are living in your own blissful world, you will be astonished by how much more just seems to magically come to you.

"Change the way you look at things and the things you look at change." - Wayne Dyer

"Get rid of clutter and you may just find it was blocking the door to what you have been looking for." - Katrina Mayer

Physical clutter is the ultimate bliss killer. I know this because I have personally experienced its effect. Clutter practically surrounded my life, my desktop, my social circle, my closet, my kitchen, my car, my calendar. It wasn't until I got fed up with being ineffective in almost every area of my life, that I knew I had to make a change. Back in '09, I decided to move across the country from Los Angeles to New York City. Through this move, I realized the power of de-cluttering my life.

I arrived to NYC with only two suitcases. Everything else I had was in storage or I had given it away. I only brought the absolute essentials because I wasn't sure how long I was going to stay. As a girl who loves a lot of things, I was terrified about this, but you know what? Life continued on. I really didn't miss anything and I had a new found sense of self as well as liberating freedom!

I felt like I had a clean slate to begin making choices and creating habits that ultimately served me in a more effective way. I became a different, more grown-up version of myself. I was able to gain massive clarity on my personal and business goals and had the home to support me in working smarter not harder because nothing was blocking my way. I had no excuses.

I'm not saying you have to sell everything and move across country to clear out the clutter in your life. I do want to tell you that by clearing out some of the clutter, you will make a massive impact on your overall wellbeing and lifestyle. Take a look around your home and if you have anything you don't absolutely love or it doesn't serve a beneficial purpose in your life, get rid of it.

Would your home say you are living your best?

Get out a pen and a notebook and make a list of the things you need to do in your home and why. You know what you need to do, you just need to do it.

Everything should have its home.

If it doesn't have a place to live, it probably doesn't belong in your home and the stagnant energy that is holding it there is most likely holding up something that wants to come into your life. If you have three tubes of toothpaste in your drawer, use them up and only keep one at a time. Be on the lookout for small signs in your home that can help determine what changes you need to make. Take regular inventory of what is in and around you and make the necessary adjustments.

For example, let's say you aren't able to get a good night's rest. You will probably want to put a little bit of money aside to buy drapes to keep the light from coming in through the window at night. You may want to toss out all of your bedding with old energy and invest in a beautiful new set or you may even need a better mattress. Perhaps you don't want to paint your walls because you are just renting and it seems like too much of a commitment. How does that reflect other commitments in your life? Are you committed to your career? Or are you just biding time and making a paycheck? Are you in a beautiful and committed relationship? Or are you stuck in a lackluster, insecure relationship just because you don't want to be alone. Your home will paint the picture of who you are being in this world. Would your home say you are living your best?

You also want to get rid of anything in your home that sucks your energy away. This doesn't have to be limited to physical objects either. Sometimes there are people you allow into your home that really just don't belong there. It could be things on TV you really don't need to be wasting your time watching. You want to guard your home like you guard your heart. Eliminate any activity, person or thing that doesn't serve you in living your best life. Energy is real. It's up to you to be an active participant in the making of your home.

Developing an abundant mindset.

Stop the 'one day' thinking. Your life is now. I always say that luxury doesn't have to be expensive. You've got to realize that life is happening NOW and you have to live it that way. This is it. We don't get another opportunity to do it again, so don't settle for the second best. Don't get down on yourself because you can't afford your dream bed or live in a high rise penthouse in Manhattan. You can make your little bungalow feel like a dream if you just give it a little bit of tender loving care. When your mindset is one of joy, abundance and gratitude, then watch how all of a sudden you attract to you all the things that you were wishing for.

I can attest to this in my own personal life. I was living in Los Angeles, in a tiny little apartment off Santa Monica Boulevard. It was far from the dream of living the high life in LA. It had '70's flooring, popcorn ceilings, and horrible wood cabinets in the kitchen, but it was all I could afford at the time. My cousin and I were living together and as much as we hated the space, he encouraged me to see beyond the dim-lit dungeon. He said, "If you want to be a real designer, then design this space and make it fabulous."

So, I did. I headed straight to Home Depot picked out some paint and began my adventures decorating our teeny little space. I was in between jobs at time due to the economic crisis, so I gave all of my attention to turning the apartment into a gorgeously modern pad. As a stroke of genius, I decided to document the process on the internet and BAM. I attracted my dream career, and a design blogger was born. Within six months I was making a part-time salary from the blog and subsequently landed a spot as a design assistant at my favorite design house in LA. In addition to that, we were throwing the best parties at our place because everyone loved it, so my relationships were thriving.

I was feeling my best and that feeling led me to make healthier choices when it came to my body. I was radiating joy. Every area of my life was impacted by the decision to make the best of what I had in the moment and everything soon improved. It all happened with such ease, it was almost like magic.

"The single greatest thing you can do to change your life today would be to start being grateful for what you have right now" - Oprah

Give excellence to all that you do.

My grandmother always showed me the importance of treating what you have with the utmost respect. Pay careful attention to what you buy and get the best you can afford. Now with the rise of online shopping and flash sites, you have no excuses. You can get anything for a ridiculously affordable price and at the touch of a button, it will be at your home in two days or less. Be sure to only pick things that you absolutely adore, don't buy just to buy. Be intentional in every purchase you make, as this is how you respect your finances and make the most of your money. You don't want to be wasteful. When you buy just to buy or because it's on sale, you may regret your choice later and regret does not encourage bliss.

Get comfortable falling in love with everything just as it is. If you can only afford a hand-me-down sofa and you don't really love it, for now cover it with beautiful pillows in your favorite color so you don't have to see much of the sofa. Take care of your life by giving your home a little bit of love and attention. Soon enough, you will have the sofa you have always wanted. In an effort to draw what you desire to you, treat what you have like it's the best there is. Don't hold back on painting your walls because it has to be the perfect color or you're just renting. Don't resist the urge to pass up on buying dishes you love because you aren't in your dream home yet. Don't not decorate or hang up art because you aren't sure how long you are going to live there. I don't care if your lease is only six months, if you spend one weekend curating your home to the best of your ability, the next six months of your life will be absolutely thrilling! When your home is right and cared for intentionally, your life will be right too!

So, why not paint your walls, hang the art, eat with the most beautiful china you own, bring in the fresh flowers, play your favorite mood music. The more you give to your home, the more your home will give to you and support you in living your life to the absolute fullest expression of who you are meant to be in this world. You deserve your dreams, so create a clean and inviting home for them to come to.

Don't waste time trying to impress others.

I'm not saying you have to throw everything out and spend thousands of dollars redesigning your home. Just making the effort in small steps can be just the things to shake up the energy in your life. Painting is one of the least expensive upgrades that makes the most impact. What is most important is that you absolutely love the wall color. Black is my favorite color and when I painted the walls to my condo black, everyone expressed their concerns. To me, it's the most magical feeling to be surrounded in a sea of noir and it feels absolutely divine. I love it and it doesn't matter how anyone else feels about it. Don't feel your home needs to be designed and compared to pages in magazines or someone else's feed on Instagram. Sure, you need to refer to the glossies for a little inspiration, just don't make decisions for anybody else but you and your family.

No matter who you are or where you are in your life, you hold the power to living an amazing life. You can design the life and home of your dreams no matter your age, relationship status, bank account or neighborhood. With just a few small but powerful changes to your home, you can absolutely transform your life, career and relationships.

Is your home in alignment with how you see yourself at your best? Does it portray what you want in your life? Does it exude success, confidence, harmony, health and all things love?

Clarifying your vision.

If you don't know where you are going, you will never get there. Before you can design your dream life you have to get crystal clear on what you want it to look like or I can tell you from experience, you will never get there. Most of the time when my clients come to me, they feel impeded by too many options. When it comes to outfitting a home, a lack of direction and endless style options can be debilitating. In an effort to get clear on just how to design your life and home, you want to decide first on your direction.

Your home and your emotions: getting to know your needs.

If you don't know what you truly are looking for when it comes to your dream life, you are not alone. A lot of people have no idea what their five year plan is, or even what they want for the next thirty days. When you aren't sure of where you want to go, a perfect determining factor to discovering your needs is paying attention to how you feel. Think about where you are and where you want to be. What do you need to do, be or have to set yourself up to get to where you want?

Perhaps you feel depressed due to a lack of funds in your bank account. You could create a nook in your home that serves as your private office to help you create your side business and double your income. One of my clients was a housewife who was tired of feeling a longing for traveling to Europe. With a husband, two dogs and three children under ten, she felt she was unable to have the time to meet her own needs, and she felt it was too selfish. Once we cleared that up (there's nothing selfish about meeting one's needs as it makes you a better and more patient parent), she started a business selling vintage furniture from her garage on Etsy. With a little bit of focus and attention, she made enough to take the whole family on a European vacation in six months.

Maybe you suffer from loneliness and desire a romantic partner or enriching friendships. So you'll need a dining room set up so you feel more confident inviting your friends over or it could be a romantic sanctuary for you and your partner to enhance the romance in your life. If you are looking to lose a little bit of weight, you may want to clean out or make updates in your kitchen that makes you want to cook healthy meals or you can even create space for a home gym. Are you longing for some solitude from the responsibilities in your life? Maybe you just need to take a long and luxurious bath and read a book. Look to what it is that you want to feel in life and see in what ways you can use your home to get you there.

What is it that you truly desire?

What is it that you truly desire?
A few questions to help you discover the life and home of your dreams.

1. Name at least five places where you feel the most joyful. This could be with certain people, doing certain things, or visiting a certain place.

2. Think about the last time in your life when you felt the most excitement. Describe your surroundings. How did it feel? Smell? What was surrounding you?

3. Imagine your dream world. Where are you? City? Beach? Castle? What are you doing? hiking? Having family over for dinner? Drinking rose on a yacht?

4. Describe your schedule for the day. How does it make you feel?

5. What are three things holding you back from your dream world?

6. What are the top five things that take up your energy right now? Are they positive influences in your life or do they drain your energy?

7. Think about this: If your walls could talk, what would they say about you? Is that who you want to be?

8. Name two places that you would love to live in. It could be a particular hotel, restaurant or even a scene from a movie. What is the style or the vibe of that space? Modern and glam? Edgy and dark? Bohemian and peaceful? Cozy and serene?

9. Determine what essence you want to be the backdrop of your lifestyle. Get clear on how it feels, what colors and smells surround you, who you are able to be in this space. Visualize it, get connected and very clear on your vision.

"The woman I was yesterday introduced me to the woman who I am today, which makes me very excited about meeting the woman I will become tomorrow" - unknown

Good vibrations.

Your home absolutely must have positive energy flowing in order for your life to propel and move forward. You can't treat your home as a place to toss your keys, sleep and shower. It's a relationship that you want to cultivate. This relationship is typically explained by Feng-Shui, a philosophical system of harmonizing everyone with their surrounding environment. I began to study Feng Shui in order to enhance my work with clients. As I began to bring elements of Feng-Shui into my design process, I noticed the shifts that were taking place in their lives almost immediately. Most people don't really get Feng-shui and are typically intimidated by it. So, I created my own fusion called Glam-Shui. Basic principles of the philosophy but with a glamorous twist. Throughout this book, I will refer to Glam-Shui and give you recipes that have worked for my clients and for me. Try them if you feel so inclined.

Every single thing inside your home carries an energy. Each color, book, photo, pillow, vase, and lamp says something about who you are. They also say something to you. As you walk around your home, pay attention to the things that surround you. How do they make you feel? I once had a girlfriend who had a beautiful Hermes pillow that was given to her by an ex- boyfriend. She absolutely loved that pillow, but it always reminded her of the old relationship, which did not make her feel good and she was always feeling so depressed because she was lonely. As hard as it was for her, I advised her to sell the pillow and get something that she also loved but with new and good energy. Reluctantly, she dumped the pillow, but soon after she met someone new and started dating again. This is an example of the magic of decluttering and changing up your energy.

Take your time and enjoy the process.

You want each room to be functional with comfortable seating, tables and trays to beautifully display the necessary items for each room. You don't need to overcomplicate this or over decorate. If you have a mess with too many things cluttering up your pad, it's not a good sign. Your schedule may be cluttered, you are probably worn out with too many commitments. Take your time determining what you want to keep, what needs to go and how you arrange your belongings. Be careful to pay attention and connect to what is filling up your home.

One client told me he and his wife had built a beautiful home and life. He shared with me that his home was perfect and pristine, and described his home like something you might see on the cover of a magazine, but if you opened any door or any drawer you would find a complete mess. I pushed him further to tell me a little bit more about himself. After a few more minutes of talking, he opened up to me that he felt like a mess, too. His wife was upset with him because he didn't want to have children, but she did. Even more than that, he felt trapped. His big secret was that he was gay, wanting to move to New York and live out his dreams, alone. He was living a perfectly happy, married life on the outside but on the inside he was miserable.

When you clear out your home, you just may discover that what you think you want may totally change. Maybe you don't want to live in the city you do now, maybe you hate your job and need a reason to leave, maybe you need to break up with a toxic friend or cut down on the alcohol. There are so many things you can uncover as you change. Be open to the change, pay attention to what you are feeling and allow yourself the time it takes to process.

VILLA NOIR — WALL COLORS

— BEDROOM

LIVING ROOM

Proper Planning

I embrace the 6 P principle: Proper Planning Prevents Piss Poor Performance. I can't remember a time where I did not hear this phrase when I did something thoughtless. My father always pressed this saying into my head and it's become one of the pillars of my business. When I work with my clients, I create a proper plan. Each and every piece comes with a rhyme and reason. In order to plan anything correctly, I like to get down to the why. The why is the reason for the space. Let's discover your why. . .

WHAT WILL BE THE MAIN PURPOSE OF THE ROOM?

IDEALLY, WHAT WILL THE ROOM FEEL LIKE?

FUNCTIONALLY SPEAKING, WHAT ARE THINGS TOP THREE THINGS YOU WANT IN THE ROOM?

From here, we can create a game plan for your space. Let's use the example of a master bedroom for a young couple. They want to feel like a B+B, an exotic vacation in Bali, an escape from the normal world. So, maybe they try including: *Velvet headboard, large scenic artwork, dim lighting.*

At this point, you can take a look at the current status of the room and make assessments as to what you need to get it to where you want it to be. Knowing what you want and what you are looking for, you can create a budget that will work for transforming your space and getting it on the path to where it needs to be. Knowing this will also help you avoid making the wrong purchases or wasting time.

Ambiance is everything.

Let's begin discussing the colors you will pick for your home. Will you be painting your walls? If not, you can bring color in through your drapes, pillows, rugs, throws, flowers, or the like. You want to nail down a color palette for your space. I like to be organized so for each room I create, I use a paint color swatch with fabrics and tactile items to create my palette. The first lady of design, Kelly Wearstler, uses vibe trays that she fills with objects that represent the theme for her intended design.

As much as I love gathering photos on the internet, I think it's much better to curate a collection of things that make a mix of the theme and vibe for the room. This way you can literally touch and feel and experience what the mood of your room will feel like before you begin to make changes.

Here are a couple of my favorite looks I used to create my personal color palette. . .

A LITTLE BIT ABOUT COLOR . .

Chromotherapy is an alternative medicine method in which therapists use color and light to balance energy wherever a person's body may be lacking; be it physical, emotional, spiritual, or mental. The premise behind chromotherapy is to harness color's wavelengths and use them to heal. After doing my research, I read that the colors that our eyes are drawn to can inspire a healing inside of us we may not even know we need.

So, when it comes to color, try not to over think or second guess yourself. Choose the colors that feel best to you.

PINK:
AFFECTION
FRIENDSHIP
OPTIMISM

GREY:
NEUTRALITY
INTROSPECTION
STILLNESS

SILVER:
OPENNESS
INTUITION

BROWN:
GROUNDING
HOME
STABILITY

PURPLE:
INTUITION
DEEP
CONNECTIONS
WISDOM

RED:
LOVE
PASSION
STRENGTH

BLACK:
PROTECTION
SILENCE
ELIMINATION

GOLD:
SUCCESS
COURAGE
SETTING
BOUNDARIES

GREEN:
PROSPERITY
HEALTH
ABUNDANCE
NATURE

BLUE:
PEACE
HOPE
PATIENCE
TRUTH

YELLOW:
CREATIVITY
COMMUNICATION
LEARNING

ORANGE:
ENERGY
VITALITY
LUCK
MAGNETISM

Dare to be bold.

Don't be afraid to use bold color on the walls. Deep hues allow the colors in furniture and accessories to pop and shine their fullest healing potential. Mixing the colors you love together is like an elixir for blissful living.

First and foremost, you'll have to decide what you want to attract into your life and what each room of your home needs to nurture. For example, are you a working girl? Do you need a home that supports strength, abundance and drive? Do you have a house filled with family members? Then you will want your home to nurture harmony, balance and security. Are you single and looking to partner up? You'll want a space that encourages spiritual awareness, with inviting and romantic harmonies.

You want to walk into your front door and feel a sense of nurturing. You want to create a mood, a vibe, a place full of happy energy that will inspire and enhance your creativity. Furniture pieces come together in such a unique way when used with color stories. Color is so powerful and so inviting you are drawn to linger around in any room where you love the color. In my home, there have been many of nights I have gone in the living room to light a candle and just be with my space. It nourishes me and it nourishes anyone who walks through my front door. As I write this very book I am sitting in my beautiful noir living room and the words are just flowing through me.

Color is like a magic elixir.

Color also can be used to enhance other areas of your life too. Take for example, your closet, what you wear has a direct correlation to your mood and the vibe and energy you give off. Your hair color, makeup, nail color, it all affects your life powerfully. What I really want you to understand from this is that you can use color to attract anything and everything you want in your life if you do it right. I always encourage my clients to keep a book with your personal color palette so you always have something to refer to when out shopping for your home.

SIX TO BLISS: My personal toolkit

One of the first columns I wrote on my blog was called "Six to Bliss." I interviewed other designers and bloggers and asked what their six essentials for domestic bliss were. While everyone had a few things that were their own personal favorites, for the most part they shared common threads.

What I found most interesting is that these common pieces of design weren't the more expensive pieces, they were the things that were the most affordable: fabric, candles, music, flowers, personal photos, natural light. These are the tools I suggest you use when trying to make your home feel a little bit more warm, cozy and nurturing. These are all things you want your home to be for you while you are on the journey of designing and living your dream life. You need a respite to support you in following your path to bliss.

Add the following enhancements to each room in your home for best results.

FABRICS. Use soft fabrics, like cottons, linens, velvets to be soft to the touch and comforting. Drapes are the very first thing I put up in any space as they are one of the most transforming factors in a space. If you look around a room and feel like it is missing something, chances are you just need some pretty curtains to be the finishing touch. I always like to match my drapes to the wall color, it makes the space feel bigger and pleasing to the eye.

CANDLES. These magical little things are like a multifaceted weapon. They look pretty, smell fabulous and create a beautiful glow. Anything and everything looks better with a little bit of candle light.

MUSIC. You want to set the mood for anything and everything. Avoid turning on the TV and play some music while you cook, while you bathe, while you are cleaning. It makes every experience much more enjoyable.

FLOWERS. I really don't think I need to say more but flowers literally bring life into your space. They are essential.

PERSONAL PHOTOS. Or even photos you took on your favorite travels. Capturing life's beautiful memories is the most gorgeous investment you can make for your home. Just be sure that each and every photo evokes a smile, something that is heartfelt and helps you feel connected.

NATURAL LIGHT. I will not move into a space with poor lighting. Well, I did once and I will never do that again. Sunlight helps you wake in the morning and moon light calms you before you go to sleep. It's one of nature's most magical experiences. It connects you to the world and we all crave a little connection, right?

God and the universe desires to give above and beyond all the we can ask or imagine. Be open and ready to receive it!

Organization and letting go.

These days, we have the power to get almost anything we want at the click of the mouse (Thank you, amazon.com!). We have instant coffee, food delivery and still we find ourselves pressed for time. Sometimes it feels like we need more than twenty-four hours in a day, am I right? Which is why organization is key to being effective in your life. Do you have stacks of unopened bills? Are there things in your fridge that are expired? Are your clothes neatly hung so you can see them? Is your jewelry all tangled together or displayed in a beautiful and organized way?

Just a few of these things can make the greatest difference in your life. You can set your home up for success just by taking a couple of extra minutes out of your day to ensure that things are in place and organize. This will inevitably free up more of your time. One of my fashionista girlfriends was always talking about the dream closets that celebrities had and how fabulous they were. While her New York apartment was teeny tiny, she took her desires into her own hands and with a few IKEA storage pieces, created the most fabulous shoe closet and placed it in her bedroom. Once she did this, she began to notice the shoes, bags and accessories she had but no longer used. Because she was so organized, it was easy for her to see what should stay and what should go. She ended up consigning those things and pocketed some serious cash. That paid for her new closet and then some. This is just an example of how a little attention to home can help you in not only your dreams but even a little more.

With so many things sucking time and attention from us, our home needs to be the place that helps us, gives to us and supports our lifestyle. For me, it's best if I spread out my jewelry so I can see it. Why waste time untangling necklaces or looking for lost earring backs? I work better opening my mail and throwing it out immediately. I keep my gym clothes organized according to type and color so it takes me about two minutes to get ready for my workouts. It's much better to feel prepared to avoid the temptation to skip the workout.

It's habits like these that make my life easier and puts me in a better position to be more effective and efficient. Say goodbye to stress and anxiety. Bid farewell to being scatter brained and exhausted. When you are organized, you establish a commitment to feeling confident, effective and powerful. This is how you get that certain glow about you. Like Henry David Thoreau says, you will be confidently going in the direction of your dreams. You'll start to see people attracted to who you are and ultimately you will serve the world by being an example. When you are a shining example of someone being all they can be, giving 100% of your best to your life, you are living the fullest expression of who God created you to be. You are a living and breathing example of what is possible in this world. This is blissful living.

How to organize memories.

When you want to hold on to your memories, but don't really have the space, the best thing to do is create boxes for specific things and then whatever fits in the box stays, the rest goes.

For example, I get the biggest kick out of old notes from high school. I kind of want to save them for my children to read one day. I have one very large three ring binder and I keep all the notes and papers I love in it. Not one thing more. The binder looks like a chic book on the outside, so it fits in wonderfully with my shelf decor.

I also find that photo albums are wonderful to keep. My secret is to buy matching albums of all the same size and shape so they look like a collection of books which makes for organized and chic decor. Keep in mind, books like these collect dust and unless you want to constantly be going around with your duster, the less of these books the better. Most

My vintage bamboo
chairs are my most
treasured family memory.

of your photos can be stored online these days. I love to keep my files kept safe on the computer or the internet. Do you remember that old question "what would you grab if your house was on fire?" Now my answer is "my hard drive."

What to do with old furniture if you must keep it.

Most old pieces of furniture look absolutely fantastic with a quick coat of paint. White is always a good look and gives off the energy of a clean slate so you can quickly get rid of old memories. I'm a girl who is incredibly sentimental and I am obsessed with my grandmother. She is just about the chicest woman I have ever known and the most domesticated diva on the planet. She nailed making a bed perfectly in under a minute. Prepare a dinner feast for twenty-five people without breaking a sweat or ruining her makeup? The woman wrote the book.

Naturally, I try to keep everything of hers that I can because the thought of her mastery keeps me going. When we were little, she had this set of bamboo chinoiserie dining chairs that sat around the formal breakfast table, which became the adult table during holidays. I was obsessed with those chairs before I even knew how stylish they were. I just always felt extremely attached to them as they represented the best part of my youth: eating beautiful meals with my whole family. Finally after years of asking, she gave them to me and I immediately had them recovered and painted them bright white. Even though they were already gorgeous and I loved the memories of them, they needed an overhaul. Over thirty years of family history is a lot of drama, fights, tense energy that every family experiences and they needed a brand new life. Now, in my home, they look breathtaking and they are ready for newer, more exciting memories. This is a fantastic example of how recovering something old and turning it into something new brings new life into your home and at the same time keeps something precious that pays respect to your family memories.

Home office: Your magnet for wealth & abundance.

Even if you don't work from home, you need a home office in order for you to be effective in life. Where and how are you organizing and paying your bills? Do you have a comfortable place to commit a few moments to balancing your bank account and tracking your finances? Even if you don't have an proper room, you want to create a beautiful desk set up where you organize your important documents, manage your finances, have a calendar you and your family can refer to, write your thank you notes, etc. This will serve as the business hub of your home. If you are in debt, looking for more income, striving to get your business off the ground, or even just trying to manage your family schedules with more ease, your home office is essential to organizing your life.

When you pay attention and respect your finances, you will automatically have a little bit of focus and energy to clear it up. I can remember when I used to be afraid of checking my credit score. I felt like I was going to into a courtroom to get cross examined or something. I didn't want to know about it at all. One day, after working with a financial coach, I swallowed my fear, poured myself a glass of wine and looked at my score. There were things on there that I didn't even know about so it forced me to take action and clear up my finances. After that, I felt a relief and a little bit more confidence about my finances. Without that subconscious fear and financial anxiety, I am able to work more effectively and feel proactive about my financial decisions.

When that energy gets cleared up, things start moving and all of a sudden you will find money available to you. So if you are needing to get a new bed, chair or invest in a better couch for your family, you have the financial confidence to plan and do so. The effect this will have on your life is unbelievable. You will begin saying yes! Most of my clients come to me with no idea of what their budget would be for their home. This is

GLAM-SHUI TIP: add a purple orchid to the upper left hand corner of your desk to attract abundance and prosperity.

actually something I have turned down clients for. It's an impractical way to go about building and designing a home. Stepping up and taking financial responsibility for yourself and your life can be the very thing that is holding you back from designing your dream life.

I am not one to teach on personal finance, and there are plenty of resources that you can access to teach you what you need to know. The books that changed my financial mindset are: *Get Rich Lucky Bitch by Denise Duffield Thomas, The Science of Getting Rich by Wallace Wattles and Master Strategy Planner by Kristi Jackson.*

While I'm not a financial expert, what I can tell you is that you need to take the time to access and manage that part of your life. If you want to create wealth for yourself, see more in your bank account, start a new business or even just get enough extra cash to buy yourself a new wardrobe, you must be in charge of your financial situation. Once you do, you will eliminate your self-doubt in that area of your life, which will help you plan for your financial future. Nothing is out of your grasp.

In what ways can you improve your relationship with your finances?

Be sure that
your home
office has a
beautiful throne
that makes you
feel powerful
while your
work.

THE
Fashion
ISSUE

CALIFORNIA STYLE

Emily Ratajkowski
shines in the season's
HEAVY METALS

I like to keep crystals and candles at my desk to
keep me feeling calm and peaceful. I also love
beautiful imagery to inspire me.

Managing stress.

Money talk can be stressful and like everything, it can be a process. If you find yourself feeling stressed while you are clearing it up, allow your home to help you in feeling better along the way.

Uplifting words. I'm big on daily affirmations and positive, inspiring imagery around the house. In your personal space, I think it is important to place photos, quotes and words that bring you back to your peaceful place. I love a photo gallery wall above a vanity space with quotes and words that keep you inspired and motivated. Keep these in beautiful matching frames to make the decor look put together and glam.

Natural Oils. I like to keep essential oils in my home to calm me when I'm feeling out of balance. Refer to the chart in section two to know which oil will suit your needs.

Fresh air. When you spend time in your home office, try opening a window to let in some natural light and a wind of some fresh air. Take a moment, focus on breathing deep and let that energy captivate you. Not only does it feel good and look good, it's super healing too.

Incorporate plants. I like orchids and succulents best in my office. They bring life and moving energy to any space. Place a cactus near your computer. It can be either big or small but the energy from a cactus helps combat the radiation that computers and other electronics give off. I know I am at my desk a lot, so this is a must for me.

only allow the
things that
ignite and
awaken you to
take part in your
everyday life!

The Body:

getting the glow

BODY = ENERGY = CHI

By transforming your environment with vibrant energy and beautiful things, your home becomes a real life manifestation of the life you really desire to live! And who doesn't want to live their life to their fullest potential? Well, maybe not all of us. Even if you aren't all gung-ho about getting your home in order, there are ways to use the good chi to truly enhance your life.

Cleansing for a fresh start.

Even after you have de-cluttered your space, you want to keep your space clean at all times. Don't let dust bunnies go hopping around or AC filters get clogged up. Your first priority in life should be your health, because if you're sick, all the money in the world doesn't matter. I like to keep my home clean, pristine and not just the surfaces. I always make sure the energy of my space is positive and up-lifting. Have you ever been to someone's house and it just feels stuffy or heavy? You really don't ever want to go back.

A simple routine for clearing out negative energy in a space is smudging. Sage is the way to go. Keep some sage on hand whenever you feel stagnant energy in your space. It's an ancient tradition that indians used to symbolize a fresh start. Each day we wake up, and it is a brand new day. We get a clean slate to create anything we want. Knowing this should allow you to let go of anything that happened yesterday that you don't feel good about. When you are living in bliss, you are forgiving of yourself, your mistakes just turn into lessons and you are rolling with the waves of life. Let yourself feel the power of new beginnings every day. When you aren't bringing old energy into your new day, you have room in your life for fresh ideas and more abundance.

Burn sage in the mornings
while reciting your
morning mantras and
affirmations.

Add plants, greenery and earth elements to the kitchen to symbolize health, balance and harmony.

Kitchen: the heart of the home

Think of your kitchen as your health headquarters. How are you treating it? Is your fridge full of beautiful foods or mostly empty with a few take out boxes? What your fridge says about you most likely correlates to the current state of your health. In order to be living to our fullest potential, we must be living at our optimal health, feeling energized and full. Pay attention to your eating habits and health routines. When you are ready to get in the best shape of your life, your kitchen is the place where you will begin.

Besides sleep, eating is one of the most consistent things we do. Most people eat at least three to five times a day. You want to do your best to eat only body nourishing foods. You don't have to go on a diet, you really can eat your favorite meals but you want to make an effort to cook them at home with fresh foods. The best part about making food at home is that you get to spend quality time with your family and loved ones. Not only should meals be beautiful and healthy but they should be spent at the dining table eating. It's not living your best that you eat while watching the television. Sure, it seems easy and relaxing but you aren't connecting to your loved ones, sorting out things that happen in your life to free up stress and worries. Eating time is a great time to conjure up feelings of gratitude and appreciation. Making it a priority to connect with the people that you love and treat your body with love is the foundation of blissful living. You want to celebrate life moment by moment to really enjoy it. Dine gloriously by drinking out of your favorite glasses and using your most special dishes. Make sure the experience excites you! I love to drink sparkling water out of a champagne flute with crisp limes. Doing small things at home in a special way is essential for your domestic bliss. It creates good energy, which is exactly what you will begin to attract.

Things to keep in the kitchen...

For a radiant glow, keep your kitchen filled with these wellness essentials.

Lemons. You should be drinking water throughout the day to keep hydrated. Flushing out toxins with water makes for the best facial ever so keep lemons on hand to dress up your water. Hot water with lemon is also an excellent way to start your day.

Apple Cider Vinegar. There is nothing that ACV can't cure. It aids in increasing metabolism, promotes healthy blood sugar levels, has antioxidant properties and improves nutrient intake.

Coconut oil. I cook with coconut oil almost daily because it's healthier than most cooking oils. It really is one of those ingredients that makes magic. You can also use it to clean your mouth, prevent wrinkles, moisturize your skin and so much more.

Avocados. You can make hair masks, top almost any meal and who doesn't love guacamole? It makes an excellent impromptu guest dish, too.

Tea. Peppermint, Chamomile, Green and Peach detox are my favorites. There is nothing that soothes the soul or the stomach like a nice cup of hot tea. Don't forget the honey.

The fundamentals of balanced living.

They say that disease begins with dis-ease, a life that's filled with struggle, which is the opposite of flow and ease. When you look at how the flowers bloom, they don't look around and compete with other flowers, they just bloom. With ease. It's important to live your life as balanced as possible in an effort to avoid the feeling of anxiety, the feeling that something is off or something is missing.

I remember when I began my business, I spent most of my time working. I was under the presumption that working harder meant I was successful. As an entrepreneur, my work day never really ends. When I realized that I was beginning to feel burnt out and wanting to give it all up and quit, I took a trip to see some old friends of mine who were living what seemed to be the easy life. Working the typical eight hours a day, they made enough money to be comfortable and take it easy. While it seemed that life was easier, it really wasn't. They were on anti- anxiety medication to numb the feelings that something was missing. Deep down, they knew they were supposed to be doing something they really loved, but they just couldn't figure out how. While I was drained spending just one night with them from all of the complaining and negative talk, I realized I was lucky to be doing something I loved, even though I was working too hard. I also discovered that neither extreme is good. It's important to strive for balance in all areas of life.

Stop and smell the roses.

To make sure that you are getting the most out of your twenty-four hours, slow down. Slow down when you chew, to prevent an upset stomach and fatigue. Slow down when you walk, as you may miss out on running into the right person, the first time. Slow down when in your talking, because you don't want to

Learn to look in the mirror and find something about yourself that you love. Feel gratitude before you walk out of your front door.

you will waste energy regretting later. When you operate from a calmer place, usually things get done right and with intention, the first time around. When we hurry through life, we miss out on milking every ounce of the bliss that comes into our world. Experiencing joy is the secret to attracting more joy, more abundance, more of everything we desire.

Creating positive habits and rituals.

What you do in your mornings determines everything about your day. Many studies have shown that in order to have a successful day, you must be intentional about your morning routine. I have always done my best to make my bed every morning but after I began to focus on my wellness, I tried creating a morning ritual that would keep me committed. It takes about twenty-one days to get in the habit of doing something, so I knew I needed something that would be fun and exciting if I was going to commit to doing it daily. I needed a personalized morning routine that would enhance my self-love, productivity, wellbeing and, ultimately, my bliss.

The first minutes in your morning should be spent investing in your self care. The second I get out of bed, I light my favorite candle, put on my deliciously soft robe, brush my teeth and make my coffee in my favorite coffee mug. Then, I get back to my bedroom and gaze out the window for ten10 long deep breaths. Next, I focus on cultivating gratitude. Scientific studies have shown the effects that gratitude has your physical well-being. Grateful people experience fewer aches and pains and they report feeling healthier than other people, according to a 2012 study published in Personality and Individual Differences. Not surprisingly, grateful people are also more likely to take care of their health. They exercise more often and are more likely to attend regular check-ups with their doctors, which is likely to contribute to further longevity. Of course, there are the stressful things in life and the things we wish weren't our reality but it's vital that for a few moments a day we set that aside. I think it's the most powerful thing to do in the morning.

When I take this time to feel grateful and breathe, plenty of thoughts come to my mind but I try to focus on all the beautiful things that surround me and give gratitude for the blessed life I lead. When you surround yourself with a beautiful home full of things you enjoy, this will serve as a helpful tool for cultivating your gratitude. Affirm the positive things you appreciate in your life. Now that I have been doing this for years, I can attest to the impact that it has had in my life and in my health.

Once I got in the habit of really indulging in these morning moments, I noticed how excited I became to get up in the morning. I couldn't wait to slip into my robe and sip my coffee while smelling my tuberose candle because it made me feel so good. When in my ritual, I feel like I am a five star luxury hotel indulging in my favorite things. This is how your home should make you feel. This also gets you in the habit of appreciating the small luxuries in your life and paying attention and being present to the HERE and NOW.

A few of my favorite prompts for creating your own morning mantras:

I AM . . .
I CAN . . .
I WILL . . .
I CHOOSE . . .
I HAVE . . .
I LOVE . . .
I CREATE . . .
I ENJOY . . .

Find a special place in your home to do your morning routine: light a candle, write in your journal, say your morning mantras.

Create healthy habits that feel good to you.

This wellness lifestyle led me to being intentional with my habits. One habit I felt instinctively drawn to do was practicing yoga. If you really want to design your dream life, I highly encourage adding yoga to your schedule. The very first time I took a yoga class, I was totally afraid to show up. I'm not a shy person but from time to time I do get intimidated by the yogi culture. I am a Capricorn, I don't like to fail at things, so seeing all the people before the class begin doing these crazy stretches just made me feel so awkward and out of place. Once the class began, the instructor could not have been more patient, sweet and open to every individual level in the class. I walked into that class with all of these thoughts buzzing around my head and these self-doubts and concerns and by the time the class was done, I had forgotten all about those thoughts in my head. Those difficult stretches not only loosened my limbs but they loosened all of those tense thoughts right out of my head. At the end of the class when she suggested we lie for a minute in silence, I balled uncontrollably. Tears just came streaming down my face. It wasn't that I was sad about anything, actually, I felt light and completely happy. I felt more self love than ever and so proud of myself that I faced my fear of going to that yoga class that day. Do that everyday and you are sure to live a more blissful life. I feel the same way about SoulCycle. Anything active that pushes you beyond your fears and comfort zone is the ultimate form of self love and a pillar of living a balanced life.

Intentionally facing fears is key to living a blissful life.

"Everything you want is on the other side of fear."
-George Addair

Embrace the green.

If you don't have plants in your home, put this book down right now and go get some. Not only do plants bring in the most beautiful hues of green into your home, they literally breathe life into you. I highly encourage houseplants because they provide healing, air cleaning, detoxifying energy, serve as insect repellant and so much more. Researches at NASA have found that house plants help purify indoor air, which is far more polluted than outdoor air. They are also said to help improve memory and concentration. So, for people like me who work from home they especially come in handy. For me, I love the way plants represent the element of nature that we all feel better when we connect to.

I wasn't always the biggest green thumb, I never really cared for a houseplant until the fiddle leaf fig tree craze. I just loved the way the bright green plant looked in decor magazines. So, I decided I had to have one for myself. To my surprise, I fell absolutely in love with it. I treated the plant like my adopted child. I would clean her leaves with a warm damp cloth, water her with extra care and move her around from time to time so all sides of her could bask in the sunlight. I really grew to love having a plant in the home. If you don't have pets or children around, its a great way to channel your nurturing needs. Plants all around just make a home feel more cozy.

If you are intimidated by the houseplant, don't fret, succulents make fantastic house plants and they are oh so easy to care for. They can be small but can go anywhere around the home and it can look incredibly chic. Everything goes with natures beautiful shades of green, no? You can place them on stacks of books, the dining table, coffee table, bedside or even the window sill.

A personal space, such a
vanity is a fantastic place
nurture your self-care.

A personal space, such as a vanity is a fantastic place to nurture your self-care.

The art of confidence.

When you look at the girls who seem to "have it all", do you ever notice there is a special air of confidence about them, that je ne sais quoi? They walk with shoulders back, chins up and with that extra pep in their step. The essential ingredients highlight a key in the foundation of a becoming a woman who has it all: confidence.

There are so many theories as to how to gain confidence. There are even books written on teaching you how to have it. So, how do you build confidence? Deep down, confidence comes from living intentionally: building, prioritizing and maintaining your self-care and self-love. Think about this, when you are headed out for a big night, what do you do? If you are like most girls I know, you go get a manicure. It's an act of self-care that makes you feel polished, poised and more together. It's about taking pride in yourself and how you approach life. When you are thoughtful enough to attend to your needs, you will be more effective and more confident when you are living your life.

The importance of self care.

I believe so strongly in the importance of prioritizing self care. It's the one key component to confidence that a LOT of people don't really talk about. Most of us are taught that having the best figure, achieving a particular status or dressing in the perfect outfit are how you gain confidence but that is NOT really the case. While those are very solid fundamentals, the root of confidence comes through knowing who you are on the inside and what many people call self-love. **So, how are we to be sure we get to know who we are on the inside and love ourselves?**

A very wise mentor of mine told me years ago, "The only person who can give you everything you need is... YOU." At first I didn't quite understand, but after a while I've learned, it's absolutely the truth. I used to always be busy, work my butt off and never really take the time to check in with myself and how I was feeling. I would sort of *numb out* through the hectic days in my life.

Silence was the catalyst for learning how to love myself.

I began paying attention to my moods, the color of my skin, how my stomach felt after eating certain foods. I would take the time to check in with how I was feeling. Each time I would have a intuitive thought or feel a different emotion, checking in would lead me to exactly what I was looking for.

How to illuminate your path...
For a little self-love, try this step-by-step guide.

Step one: Define your feelings. Get alone with yourself, take a moment to describe your current state of feelings. Are you angry, sad, anxious, frustrated, confused?

Step two: See where you are uncomfortable. Once you locate your feeling, try to understand your reasoning behind that. Don't fight it, just allow it to be.

Step three: Locate what is draining you or sucking your energy. Stop doing it immediately. If something you are working on isn't working, put it down for a while. If its a person in your life, try taking some space. Don't force it.

Step four: What is currently giving you energy or excitement? For me, it could be a new project, a trip to Barnes and Nobles or meeting an uplifting, positive friend for coffee.

Step five: Put a self-care ritual or routine in place. Take a nap, take a long bubble bath, meditate, get a facial, take a hot yoga class, pick up a bundle of fresh flowers and arrange them, read books that enrich the mind instead of t.v. shows, go outside for a long walk and connect with nature, watch a movie that makes you cry, redecorate a nook in your home, light a delicious candle, journal your feelings, write someone a love letter, do anything that you absolutely love doing and do it immediately.

Step five: Continue going in that direction. Follow your bliss. You'll be feeling full of love and confident in no time.

Learn to love yourself.

Once I realized that taking the time to invest in what I put in my body, how I treat it, how I take care of my health and skin, it started to really serve me. I had to learn to slow down, be more intentional in everything I do, pay attention to how I prioritize my well-being. I've noticed that as I was being more intentional in my self care as well as paying more attention to my feelings and to my needs, I've developed a much better sense of self. Learning to trust yourself is key to becoming a better decision maker and allowing your intuition to be your guide. As you take the necessary steps for prioritizing your self care, it will feel a little more natural to fall in love with yourself.

So, for those of you who think you shouldn't be spending money on great skin care, healthy shampoo and conditioner, natural bathroom products, fresh flowers weekly, lavish candles and delicious bath towels. . .I'm hoping to change your mind and nudge you to get out of your comfort zone. I understand if you can't afford spending hundreds of dollars at the spa, so if that is you, why not create the ultimate, pampering, spa at home? Luxury doesn't have to mean expensive.

I've noticed that when I am prioritizing self care in all areas of my life, I do things with a greater level of excellence. I take time to build myself up so that I feel better about myself and the work I do. I find that when I do so, I work smarter, not harder. I am intentional and effective in each and every activity, which allows me to be more present. Overall, I've noticed the largest changes in my relationships and in my work.

In order for me to be sure to prioritize my self care, I stick it into my calendar and make every effort not to blow off my personal needs. I highly encourage you to develop this skill, connect with your body, treat it like a temple, feel your feelings, *follow your bliss.*

Shopping for fresh flowers in the afternoon has always been one of my favorite ways to treat myself and my home with a little extra love and attention.

feel your feelings, follow your bliss!

Scentual healing.

One of my first memories of smell was about the time I was five and I remember waking up one morning and yelling, "It smells like Christmas!". That was my first recollection of scent and how impactful the scent was for me. After that, I was never the same. I have been fascinated by smells and how smell is tied to memory and experience. For that reason, I'm always paying attention to decorating for the senses. I want my home experience to be joyous and blissful so smell is never forgotten in my space. Not only does it have to be beautiful, I want you to enjoy each and every breath you take when you are in my home. When you leave my home, it is so important to me that you enjoyed how lovely it smells. Fragrance is healing.

Whether it's musk that gives you beautiful memories of your special time with your grandfather or lavender to calm your nerves, sense of smell plays a powerful role in our lives and our wellbeing. Candles and oils play a vital role in my repertoire of scents. Not only do candles provide a glow and set the mood, they also can be helpful to enhance your sensory experience and energy. Lavender will always be great for calming me before bed so I can get proper rest. I also keep grapefruit oil to add to my water before my workouts because it invigorates me. I am a huge fan of Doterra oils and have an oil diffuser in the home. Whenever I need to feel more of something, I use the appropriate oil for whatever it is I am feeling. This brings balance to my body and my energy.

Always light a candle when you get home.

My grandmother was the best model of this in my life. She taught me to light a candle in the entryway, just incase guests stop by they will always enjoy coming in. She taught me to spray my bedding with beautiful linen sprays and to this day, I teach everyone who comes into my life to do the same. Even if you just spray a quick dash of Febreeze to your bedding in the morning, this simple move makes getting into bed each night that much more delightful. I have sprays for my under garments, sprays for my sofa and blankets and I even splurge on beautiful smelling counter sprays. You want your clothes to smell fresh and beautiful when you wear them, so be sure your laundry detergent smells clean and fresh. My favorite are the lavender scented ones. Just the other day while doing hot yoga, I was thoroughly enjoying the lovely lavender aroma of my yoga clothes.

I also like to keep my perfumes collected together in a tray on my vanity. It looks chic and provides me with easy access to beautiful smells. That way, I can walk around my home or out the

door and feel fresh and confident. Try to keep beautiful smelling lotions and oils for your skin to stay nourished., I also like to keep hand lotion on my bedside table to keep my hands moisturized and smelling good before bed. When I do this little ritual, I take a little moment to really take it in and enjoy the smell. These are little luxuries that make all the difference to our lifestyle.

A LITTLE BIT ABOUT OILS . .

Aromatherapy is the practice of using the natural oils extracted from flowers, bark, stems, leaves, roots or other parts of a plant to enhance psychological and physical well-being.

The inhaled aroma from these "essential" oils is widely believed to stimulate brain function. Essential oils can also be absorbed through the skin, where they travel through the bloodstream and can promote whole-body healing. I like to use essential oil mixes throughout my home. Here are a few recipes I enjoy:

IN THE BATHTUB:
2 DROPS OF
PEPPERMINT

IN MY WATER BOTTLE:
5 DROPS OF GRAPEFRUIT
1 DROP OF FRANKINCENCE

IN THE DIFFUSER:
2 DROPS OF LAVENDER
1 DROP OF GRAPEFRUIT
4 DROPS OF EUCALYPTUS

IN MY ROOM SPRAY:
7 DROPS OF LAVENDER
3 DROP OF YLANG YLANG
2 DROPS OF ROSE

Curate a capsule wardrobe to look like a
boutique at home so you feel fabulous
while getting ready in the morning like
Cara Alwill Leyba.

Closet: your magnet for more

Picture this: you are walking down the street to grab a coffee in an outfit that fits you fabulously and makes you feel good about yourself. The fabric just feels like a dream, your outfit fits like a glove and makes you feel like a million bucks. Your shoes are beautiful and comfortable and your sunglasses are a complete reflection of your personality. This is what your clothes can do for your confidence. You don't even have to have a closet full of expensive clothes, you just want to curate a closet for yourself that feels like a dream. Only let in the things that fit you where you are in life right now. Don't buy things just because of a label or shoes that are too small. Try not to hold on to anything that doesn't fit your or outdated pieces. That will totally kill your confidence.

Once your closet is empty, now is the time to start curating it with your most favorite things.

It's important that I keep my closet looking like a fabulous little boutique. This ensures that it is empty enough to see every garment so I can get ready with ease. I use black velvet hangers so everything looks matching and polished. Make sure your clothes are stored properly and cared for so that when you go to wear them, they are flawless. It doesn't take a lot to have a brilliant closet, you just have to pay a little extra   attention to how you display and store your wardrobe. When things are easy to find, it's easier to get dressed in the morning. You don't want to be fumbling around and rushing things, throwing something together last minute. If this sounds like your routine, I highly suggest making some changes in your closet.

Mirrors are the secret weapon.

When your closet in edited and there is room, energetically you are telling the universe that you have room for more! Mirrors are the secret weapon for more: confidence, clothes and charisma. When we were, little my father always told us to look in the mirror and love yourself. That was how he helped build our self confidence. To this day, we all make ourselves practice that. So from a young age, I learned to love mirrors. If there is an empty wall in a house, I would throw a mirror up in a heartbeat. Another reason I am all about mirrors is because they are a secret key to moving energy. Mirrors reflect whatever energy comes in times two, especially light, so if you are in a smaller space or a darker space, mirrors work wonders. So, keep a full length mirror in your closet and make sure at all times you are feeling and dressing your best. Your beautiful, clutter free closet will now make room for more to come into your life.

In certain Feng-Shui philosophies, mirrors are referred to as the aspirin of Feng-Shui and can totally cure most things. If something feels off in a space, hang a mirror. Mirrors bring a sort of flowy, water element to a home therefore adding calm and refreshment. There are a few caveats to this, don't place one to where it faces your bed, or it can disturb your sleep. Also, try not to place them facing each other directly, that can be weird vibes. For the most part, if you are feeling any area of your home is dull or needs some life and good energy...just add a mirror. As many of you know, I'm a gold girl so I am all about the gold mirror. Gold is also said to symbolize wealth and enhance luck and prosperity in the home, so why not add a little bit of that energy in your home too?. I have a huge gold mirror sitting on my desk in my home office. Hello, lady luck!

Where can you add a mirror in your home?

Restoration Hardware knows the power of mirrors. The grand entryway staircase is lined with beautiful gold ones.

when you
love
what you have
you have
every thing
you need.

The Soul:

falling in love with your life

Nurture your relationships.

Earlier in the book, you took a few moments to think about what you really want in your life. If you are having trouble dreaming up the life you want, we can start with just solving some of the situations in life that take you away from living in bliss. One of the most common feelings I find for clients is battling loneliness. Sure, no one really wants to admit it but these are the loneliest times we have ever experienced. Most of us live behind our phones or computers. Long gone are the days of phone calls and face-to-face communication. Relationships with loved ones and even our relationship with ourselves can be the most important thing to nurture in our lives. It's time for us to understand our need for connection and companionship and make it a priority. It's especially important in our home.

Embracing Entertaining

In the home, this begins in the living area. What is the current status of your dining room and living room. Is it inviting? Are you prepared for having friends or family members over? If not, this is one of the causes for your loneliness. You want to set the stage for inviting the people you love to experience building memories with you. You want to bring beautiful energy and life into the space with the personalities of those that uplift and encourage you.

In other words, you want to set your home up to support you in being a fabulous hostess. You don't have to have a formal dining room or even a guest bedroom to make feels guests feel right at home. The important thing about hosting is connecting with others. Be sure to practice the art of listening. Positively engage in the conversation, leave the negativity out. If there is any conflict in the home, quickly aim to resolve the problem, so as to not have any lingering negativity.

Something as small as pouring OJ into a beautiful pitcher makes a world of difference.

Hosting with purpose.

In order to ensure a successful evening with your loved ones, you want to create a positive and uplifting environment for everyone involved. Life can bring difficult stresses and formidable challenges.

Make your home an easy place to let the worries fade away. As guests arrive or loved ones come home, immediately offer a comforting drink upon arrival. Whether its a glass of wine or cup of chamomile tea, surprise your guests with the best glassware you have. No occasion is too simple for breaking out your beautiful crystal glasses. Your guests are sure to notice the extra bit of effort you put in and it will have them feeling extra special. As Mother Theresa says, "Let no one come to you without leaving feeling better." This will surely do the trick.

I always think that unique ways of serving are best. Create themes for different evenings. I always like to cater to the interests of each of my friends. For example, those who are interested in travel could each bring something interesting from there favorite adventures. Each guest can take turns talking about their adventures. This makes for such a fun evening. Ask each guests to bring their own dish or dessert to go along with the theme. Wine tastings can also be a blast with the right appetizers going around and can illicit very interesting conversation. You can even turn something super simple into an extraordinary experience. If you are having an asian inspired meal, break out the chopsticks and discuss the flavors. Encourage your guests to really take in all of the aspects of the meal. Make it a fun activity. I am huge on hosting game nights. I keep multiple games in my kitchen to entertain and keep the conversation flowing. Book discussions can be fun, too.

One of my favorite evenings at my home is a good movie or television night. I am obsessed with period shows like Game of Thrones or Marie Antoinette. Setting up the dinner table according to the set decor makes it that much more fun. Regularly hosting in this way keeps you engaged in your community, feeling connected and totally blissful.

I can remember my first apartment in NYC was less than 300 square feet. Not much room for entertaining, let alone room to cook. I did, however, purchase two large, comfortable chairs that sat at the edge of my bed with a small cocktail table that had just enough room for a table for two. I made sure to equip my space for out of town guests to hang and feel at home. I always had guests in that tiny little space and the memories we built in that small space are those that will last a lifetime. It doesn't matter what you have, make the best of it and make it work. Have enough glasses for guests to have coffee, tea, wine, champagne and water. These are my essentials. Have enough plates and silverware that you can serve in style. Set up a dining situation that is inviting, have candles, flowers and beautiful linens. Make sharing a meal a memorable and enjoyable experience. There have been plenty of times with my clients where I end up teaching them how to prepare and set up a

basic meal to entertain. Or, these days, you can run up to Whole Foods and grab a quick meal to go which is fine. It's all about the presentation that goes the distance. Bring it home or order take out, just be sure it feels special, don't use the plastic forks.

"Let no one ever come to you without leaving better and happier."
-Mother Theresa

Giving thanks.

One of the most important things you can do to ensure blissful living is to always be gracious. As a guest, hostess or any other situation in life, a handwritten note is always appreciated. Keep beautiful stationary stocked in your home office or vanity with a beautiful pen. Light a candle and take the time to write beautiful thank you notes to your guests and loved ones. I used to love getting little notes in my lunch box as a child, its a small gesture but it makes the world of difference.

Good etiquette will always be sure to foster harmonious relationships in your life. I highly encourage you practice this in your business too. One of my business coaches always taught me the importance of over giving. When you over deliver on who you are personally or professionally, you are teaching others you are intentional and of high value. In return, you will find that people are eager to work with you or be around you because you are committed to good values.

How are you communicating your values and ethics in your relationships? Are you committed to integrity and abundance or are you portraying lack and competition?

It's very important to take stock of the way you are showing up in your life and in your personal and professional relationships. It's never too late to make an excellent lasting impression. Begin being committed to always giving excellent service and hosting with passion and love.

Creating a blissful ambiance.

The connection to our spirit is the most important connection we can have. Think of your home as the physical expression of your soul and decorate it accordingly. There are many things we face in life and your home can keep you connected and grounded to your authentic self. It can be like a best friend.

You want to use your five senses when decorating to be sure that everyone who enters your home has an enjoyable experience. Be sure there is comfortable seating for people to sit back and relax. If you live in cooler climates, have throw blankets sitting around and don't hesitate to light the fire for your guests. In the bathrooms, be sure the soaps smell good and there are clean hand towels to use. Keep your art visually appealing and pleasing to the eye. Candles, flowers and cleanliness are all important so that your home smells inviting and fresh. I keep bowls with nuts and candies in my home so if someone is hungry, they can grab a quick nibble. Last but not least, make sure the music is soothing and fun. Everyone loves good music.

Artwork shows off your personality.

Make it a priority to choose artwork that connects you to your soul. Don't just throw up any old piece. Use images that illicit conversation and inspiration. Perhaps a place you often dream of or photography from your most favorite adventures. To have your home be captivating and brilliant, make sure that the artwork on walls portrays who you are to the very core. This will let your guests see the real you, a more intimate side of you that they may not know about. The authenticity of your artwork will enhance your relationships by opening a window to your soul for all to see.

I love taking photos of doors in NYC. My favorites hang in my home.

Where and how you hang artwork sets the tone of the room so be sure it fits the vibe you want to experience. In the bedroom, you want to use images that inspire relaxation and romance. You may want to try placing a large landscape image across from your bed so you can fall asleep to the breathtaking view. Choose an image that sends you off beautifully into your dreams. In the bathroom, I like simple artwork. I always opt for nude sketches or botanicals of some kind. In the dining room, I like to encourage people to place dramatic artwork that stirs up conversation. Anything that interests you will do.

Turn up the volume.

I don't know about you, but I love music. When I go to a concert with music that I love, my spirit just lights up. I'm feeling a groove, I can dance like no one is watching and my five-year-old self is totally expressed. Give your home some of your soul and play music that you love. Create the soundtrack of your life. I can remember when I moved into that first apartment in NYC, and I was all by myself, I turned on my favorite music and instantly felt at home. When I entertain my family and friends for dinner parties, it's music that makes us start dancing, laughing and having the time of our lives. Music is a universal language that allows us to connect to others easily. If you are feeling lonely, play music to connect you with your soul. I can attest to many times needing a good cry and nothing could get it out of me like music. I love old Motown R+B, especially Otis Redding who always makes me feel connected and soulful.

For my morning routine I play a zen meditation playlist with calming and relaxing music that gets me in the spiritual zone. Everyone loves when I play it at home, it creates a calming environment for everyone to enjoy and be silent. When I am hard at work, classical music works best for me to really get me in the zone. My sister knows when that music is on not to disturb me. It inspires her to get to work too.

When something
beautiful
captures your
attention,

bring it
home!

When I get home from a long and tiring day, I like to hear soft piano sounds to relax. It's better to turn on the music than the television to detox your mind after a rough day. Music that sounds good to you fills your brain with neurohormones which affect your levels of dopamine in a good way. Have you ever tried exercising without music? It just isn't the same. I can't quite focus without something to stimulate my mind into action. Same thing goes for cleaning house, cooking meals, taking a bath, painting your walls, etc. It can make your home experience so much more blissful.

Let there be light.

Good lighting is the key to creating the right mood. In the mornings natural light is the best way to wake up to the world. I like to be sure to have the curtains pushed back in beautiful velvet ribbon before bedtime so that with the morning light I awake naturally.

You want to equip your home with proper lighting for any situation. In the evenings, I like it soft and moody. I am not a big fan of overhead lighting. I think table lamps and floor lamps are always key. So, if you do have overhead lighting or a chandelier, its best to have it installed with a dimmer to adjust the light throughout the day. One of my favorite looks is low lighting behind plants and objects. It highlights the nook and gives off the perfect glow.

Candles are also a fantastic source for lighting. I like to keep candlesticks in every room, just incase I feel the desire to relax but still have a little bit of light. Candlelight also makes for the best personal glow. Everyone looks good in candlelight. Pink lightbulbs are great for the bedroom and cast a soft and romantic glow. You can adjust your lampshades too. In the winter, I like dark lampshades with gold lining. It just makes the walls at night sing. In the warmer months, linen beige or white lampshades can allow for more light, especially on those warm Summer nights.

"close your eyes and *imagine* the best version of you possible. That is who **you** really are."

- c. assaad

The Art of coming home.

There is no better feeling than the comfort of home. No matter where you live or who you live with, life will seem as if it is missing something if you don't have a place you call home. This looks different for everybody. For some, it may be hotels and for others it may even be an airstream. What is important is that you have a sacred space that you retreat to at the end of your day. Coming home should feel blissful, exciting and comforting.

Home should be your safe space.

When you walk through the front door at the end of your day, your home should welcome you with open arms and feel like a long hug. You want to feel at ease, at peace, and everything surrounding you should make you smile. From the way it smells to the things you see and what you hear, all of it should make you feel amazing about who you are.

Home is the place where you can take off the troubles of the day and leave them outside. It should be your sanctuary for transforming into the magical creature that sits inside your soul. You should feel free to do whatever you choose and whatever makes you feel good. You shouldn't be ashamed or afraid to be the best possible version of yourself at home.

If you live with others, you should allow and encourage the same for them. Let everyone in your home express their inner child within the walls of your home. Leave life's troubles outside. Bake cookies, watch silly movies, have a dance party, play games, dress up in costumes, etc. Don't allow your home to be so serious. Home should be the place where you feel the most wild and free. If this isn't how it is, things should change immediately.

Dress up for your dreams.

Do you ever notice how little kids get that special comfort from their favorite blankie? That's me with my robe. It's like a wonder woman cape to me. I feel fabulous and glamorous when I wear my robe at home. Do you dress up for your home the way you dress up for your life? If not, you absolutely should. I have a whole wardrobe for the home, including beautiful robes for every season, a couple pairs of silk pajamas and a beautiful apron for cooking.

If you find yourself, tossing on old ratty clothes when you get home because they are comfortable, it is time to update your home wardrobe.

If you can't tell by now, your home is the most important place you spend your day. Dress up for yourself, your husband, your children, dress up for your dreams. Show the world you are ready to live in excellence. This will not only impact your life, it will impact those who surround you too. I only ever remember my grandmother looking fabulous and she rarely left the house. She would always wear this blue silk floral kimono robe. As kids, we would watch as she sat at her vanity and put on her makeup in her fabulous robe, and we were intoxicated by her. She always had a full house and with six children and their families at the house, and her hands were always full. I never once saw her not looking fabulous, whether she was in a nightgown, robe or a beautiful caftan while serving sandwiches to us by the pool. She prioritized looking her best at all times, not just for herself but for the people she loved. To this day, I especially love my robe because it makes me feel like that - fabulous. When I prepare for bed, I want to feel luxurious and comfortable and a beautiful robe will provide you with just that. Dress at home in your most fabulous lounge wear and you will feel better about yourself than ever before.

Don't be shy at home. Dress
in your most fabulous lounge
wear items.

When you get home from a long day, try lighting a beautiful smelling candle as soon as you walk in the door. Go change into your most fabulous home wear. Turn on some soothing music. Open a window and let in some fresh air. Take a long bubble bath or how shower and wash away the worries of your day. Now that you have made it home, this is the time to really nurture and indulge yourself so that you can give the best of who you are to everyone else.

Lose your mind. Find your soul.

Take the time to unwind. Typically I enjoy using essential oils when I first get home. I put some drops of lavender in the bathtub or make myself a hot towel with eucalyptus for an invigorating moment. I take a few long, deep breaths to center myself. Resist the urge to turn on the television or the news. Tune into your self and your feelings. Allow the space for others in your home to do the same.

Curate your spa at home.

Time spent in the bathroom should be absolutely the most blissful. Add a chair or stool in your bath that gives you comfort while you are putting on your lotion and other products. Keep candles, fresh flowers, pretty pictures, crystals and anything that reminds you of a spa. Warm fluffy towels and super comfortable bath mats are essentials in any bathroom. I've always loved reading books or magazines in the bath, so keep those nearby too. Take your time to enjoy and nurture this part of your home.

Don't you just love the feeling of getting into a deliciously made bed feeling fresh and clean? I love to take baths before I go to bed and I literally imagine myself washing away the disappointments of the day.

There will always be things we don't get to on our to do lists or people we forgot to call back but we have to be gentle with ourselves, because we are doing the best we can. When you are aiming to live a better life, pay attention to the small details of every experience and don't rush through the process. Light some candles, play some classical music, use your best and fluffiest towels, intoxicating bath salts. Even if you can't find time in the day to get to everything, prioritize your end of the day ritual to prepare you for getting well rested. This will ensure you wake up the next morning ready to make the most of the day.

Meditation and journaling.

Your home is the perfect place to strengthen your connection with self and God and it provides a beautiful backdrop to cultivate your spirituality. When you are feeling full like your cup runneth over and aligned with your most joyous self, you can't help but radiate bliss. Your relationships will be transformed because love will be pouring out of you. No matter where I am, I find a place to meditate and pray. Taking deep breaths is the secret ingredient to a blissful life. Meditation reduces stress, improves concentration, benefits cardiovascular and immunity health and the best part of all, it is hands down, the best tool you have for anti-aging. You don't have to be a monk or super hippy either. I am all about feeling glamorous when I meditate. I have beautiful silk pillows in a corner of my bedroom with a comfortable chair where I meditate and journal. I have a little table with beautiful crystals, candles and flowers. All the things that make me happy and feel spiritual. It's my own little personal altar and I suggest you do what feels good to you. Just make sure to carve out a little space in your home where you feel is yours and only yours. Everyone in the home needs their personal space to meditate and pray. All you have to do is quiet your mind, pay attention to the thoughts that run your mind. I personally was taught to imagine each thought as if it was passing through like on the stock market screen in Times Square. Just allow them to come and go with no resistance. You just observe what your thoughts are and while doing so take deep, long breaths that you feel from head to out. As you exhale, just imagine all negativity just flows right out of you.

If you have piles of laundry and see things you aren't particularly thankful for when you look around, take that moment to exhale, accept it, as it is and make a commitment to get it done. If you are stressed due to a lack of ability to pay a bill, pray for the universe to show you an opportunity.

Break out a pen and paper.

Typically after I meditate, I spend some time journaling. I find when I am journaling, I am feeling most connected. It's just what I love to do. I love pens and markers and beautiful journals. I always have since I was a little girl. There have been times where I have just written my thoughts and prayers out and literally God will answer me through my own writing. I'll read back what I wrote and have had a total epiphany. There are so many benefits to journaling. Studies have shown it has been beneficial in improving your communication skills because you can organize and reflect on your thoughts and feelings. When you have a high emotional intelligence and strong communication skills, your relationships will flourish. You will connect better at work with co-workers, be direct with your family and loved ones and thrive in your romantic relationships. I love to journal right after I meditate and if I need to journal my day out at night, I do so in bed right before I go to sleep. It's a fantastic practice to get in the habit of before you go to bed because you can literally take everything that happened during the day and dump it out on paper before you sleep.

You will connect better at work with co-workers, be direct with your family and loved ones and thrive in your romantic relationships. I love to journal right after I meditate and if I need to journal my day out at night, I do so in bed right before I go to sleep. It's a fantastic practice to get in the habit of before you go to bed because you can literally take everything that happened during the day and dump it out on paper before you sleep.

Never underestimate a good nights sleep.

Sleep is a spiritual experience. It fuels your body in the most incredible ways. Even Arianna Huffington wrote a book on the impact sleep has on our lives. Ongoing sleep deficiency is linked to an increased risk of heart disease, kidney disease, high blood pressure, diabetes, and stroke. So why would we not take that seriously? Your bedroom should be equipped with the things that keep you rested while your body gets the rejuvenation and recovery it needs. Make sure your bedroom has soft lighting and soothing images that don't aggravate you before you fall asleep. I like to keep soft linens, fluffy pillows and blankets to feel like I am sleeping on a cloud.

Layer bed with your favorit
fabries so that going to slee
feels divin

Bedroom: your magnet for love

I have always had the most respect for my bedroom. Even when I was in college, I would buy the most expensive sheets I could afford because I wanted my bed to be the ultimate sleeping experience. Your bedroom should serve as your sanctuary to not only provide the space for self care but for harmony in your soul. Your walls should be moody, lighting should be dim and blankets should be soft and comfortable. Invest in the best you can afford to sleep on. I always urge my clients to buy fabric covered headboards and have matching nightstands. Feng-Shui advises that you should have matching nightstands to keep the balance and harmony in your relationships, so the energy is equal.

Attract your soulmate.

One of my most favorite clients ever, contacted me about re-decorating her master bedroom. She was trying to get over a breakup and move on and she wanted to create a beautiful bedroom to attract her soulmate to her. We painted her walls a beautiful, moody lavender, hung a gorgeous crystal chandelier with a dimmer, put up taffeta silk drapes. I made sure that she had matching nightstands with crystal lamps and only hung artwork that said the words love or images of romance. Shortly after this, she called me to let me know that after her home makeover, she felt a new sense about her. She was feeling more feminine and fabulous than ever, so much so that within a few months her ex came crawling back to her. Now, they are engaged to be married. I know it sounds a little crazy but I have tons of stories just like this. If you are wanting to enhance your relationships with self, romantic partners or loved ones, the bedroom is the place to start.

How to attract the one. . .

or just improve the love you already have using Feng-shui principles.

Clear out old energy. Get rid of anything that ties you to past relationships. Momentos, photos, letters, etc.

Locate the Marriage and Relationships bagua. Standing at your bedroom door, find the far right hand corner of the room. Use this corner as the love hub. Place anything that symbolizes love and romance in this corner. Pink things, romantic artwork, anything in pairs.

Bring in life. Pink roses and plants with heart shaped leaves are best for bringing in new loving energy to your bedroom.

What is on your walls? Only place art in the bedroom that encourages love and romance for you. Don't put family photos or anything to do with children in there. Keep it romantic. Perhaps images of a romantic city you want to travel to would work best your the bedroom.

Don't work in the bedroom. Keep your bedroom free of anything stressful or work related. No computers or printers.

Encourage harmony. Light candles, place matching nightstands on either side of the bed, keep lighting low.

Think pink. Place a pink himalayan salt lamp in the relationship corner. It is said to be a powerful magnet for love.

An example of a *glam-shui* love and relationship corner. Have fun with it, make it as beautiful as your dreams.

Just say yes!

When you have designed a life and home that lights you up, you will now be in what I call the 'bliss zone'. It is in this space where doors will start opening up for you. It's important to be open and aware of the opportunities that life throws your way. Walk through the doors of those opportunities. Follow your bliss.

In my own personal journey, I made the decision to only go in the direction of what truly feels good to me. If a design job doesn't feel right for me, I won't take it, even if it means I could make good money. While I could aim for creating spaces that make covers of magazines, I made my business more about designing spaces for my clients personal bliss. When I don't feel good about a business collaboration, even though it seems like a fab opportunity, I won't take it. Instead I decided to keep the faith that when one door closes, another one opens. The opportunity that feels good to you is the right opportunity.

Now I don't mean that there will be no challenges. Struggles and hardships are our best teachers. That's part of the beauty of it all. I want to encourage you to just say yes when an opportunity feels right. You must say yes, even if it seems unthinkable, too good to be true or intimidating. It may take a little bit of work but if you daily take actions to follow your bliss, you will be exactly where you need to be for everything you want to come to you.

I think the most important story of all is the story behind this book. A few years ago while sitting in post meditation journaling, I got the idea for this book. I got the name, the idea and I uncovered my personal mission in this world. Not only do I want to make the
world a more beautiful place one interior at a time, I want to share what I have learned about designing your dream home and life. I

learned how one is not separate from the other. I just couldn't get the words to make sense or come together for this book. It has been sitting inside of me for over three years. Ask many of those who are closest to me and they will tell you they know the premise of this book and they have just been waiting for it to come out.

It wasn't until I finally made the move into my dream home, set it up exactly how I wanted it to be, applied all of the practical glam-shui tools I have learned, worked on my wealth consciousness, began watching what I put into my body, committed to my yoga practice and took time away from work to nurture my relationships with those who I love. I immersed myself in doing things that made me feel blissful like arranging flowers, making vision boards, attending concerts, burning candles. It was then that the words in this book were able to pour out of me. I am so grateful that I finally am able to share it with you.

This book was a commitment to my own dreams. Financially, I am more abundant than ever before, and each year, even as I get older, I feel younger and more vibrant. I am experiencing the most rich and fulfilling relationships and now I am living in bliss. The book is my anthem cry that YOU TOO can design the life and home of your dreams. I am committed to your dreams. I want you to win!

I hope you will take the words I have shared with you and apply them to your life and watch for your own abundance and increase. No increase is too small and no ones is better than another. It's yours and yours alone. You no longer have to ever compete for anything because what is yours is only for you.

So what are you waiting for? Go out and get it!

About the author
ASHLINA KAPOSTA
ASHLINA IS AN INTERIOR DESIGNER, BLOGGER, AUTHOR & MENTOR

Ashlina made her mark in the world with her interiors blog, The Decorista. After moving from Los Angeles to New York City, and a desire to make the world more beautiful, she founded her design firm Ashlina Kaposta Interiors.

Ashlina's passion has created an online destination for anyone looking to learn how to live an inspired and glamorous lifestyle. Her focus is on secrets of domestic bliss, finding luxury in the details and changing the way you feel about coming home.
With her award winning interior designs, online mentorship programs and spiritually focused magazine, Ista Magazine, she is looking to inspire and equip women with the tools for designing a beautiful life.

To connect with Ashlina visit
www.ashlinakaposta.com
Facebook: @thedecorista
Twitter: @thedecorista   Instagram: @thedecorista

About the illustrator
WENNA PRIVÉ
WENNA IS A FASHION ILLUSTRATOR

Her love of old-world elegance from a bygone era influences her feminine illustration style. The glitzy world she creates evokes nostalgic feelings of classic glamour.

Wenna formally studied Creative Direction at the Private Academy of Art University in San Francisco. She then moved to Los Angeles after landing work in Fashion PR.

When the city was asleep, she would stay up late at night to sketch the exquisite gowns and creations from designers she admired. Her keen eye for fashion and attention to detail led to invaluable opportunities such as styling for red carpet events and exclusive photo shoots, as well as working countless fashion shows. Deciding to leave her life in Los Angeles to travel abroad, Wenna continued drawing and painting whenever she could.

She traveled back to Paris, London, and New York, keeping her sketchbook constantly in hand. The stunning architecture, rich history and beauty of these destinations further sparked her true love for drawing and couture.

She took the leap, high heels first, discovering illustration as a way to share her passions.

Made in the USA
Columbia, SC
13 December 2017